P9-EDY-339

# BRYCE CANYON
NATIONAL PARK

A VISUAL
INTERPRETATION

Essay
by
Nicky Leach

Dec. 19, 1995

Hey, Meleda!
I looked, but I didn't
see any blushing brides
in any of the pictures!
Thanks for being part of
one of the highlights of
my year. What an adventure!
Thanks also for being a great
friend, roommate + psychologist.
Happy Birthday, '95!
Love, Jenni

# SIERRA PRESS, INC.

# BRYCE CANYON
## NATIONAL PARK

### A VISUAL INTERPRETATION

Essay
by
Nicky Leach

Spires and hoodoos seen from Inspiration Point.

Ponderosa pine growing between fins in Queen's Garden.

Bryce amphitheater seen from near Sunrise Point.

FRONT COVER PHOTO: Thor's Hammer seen from the Navajo Loop Trail.
BACK COVER PHOTO: Bryce amphitheater, seen from Bryce Point, winter sunrise.

ISBN O-939365-42-1

Copyright 1995 by The Sierra Press, Inc.

All rights reserved. No part of this book may be reproduced in any form without written permission from the publisher, except by a reviewer who may quote brief passages or reprint a photograph.

Printed in Singapore.
First Edition: Spring 1995.

# ACKNOWLEDGEMENTS

We would like to take this opportunity to thank the many photographers who made their imagery available to us during the editing of this title. While no single image can effectively replace the actual experience of being there, we believe the visual story told by the images contained in this volume do tell the story of seasonal change and process more effectively than what the visitor would experience while on vacation.

We would also like to thank Susan Colclazer and the Interpretive Staff of Bryce Canyon National Park, as well as LaKay Quilter, Paula Henrie, and their staff at the Bryce Canyon Natural History Association, for their assistance in the creation and formation of this book—Thank You!

# DEDICATION

This book is a visual tribute to the insight of those few who saw the wisdom of setting aside such a tract of land for the future, without regard for personal gain. That the National Park Service and its components have become models for more than 130 countries from around the world is all the proof that is necessary to confirm their wisdom. We can only hope our own use is consistent with this wisdom and in no way contributes to the degradation of this most extraordinary legacy.

In this spirit, let us all pledge to continue to work, and sacrifice, for the greater good of places such as Bryce Canyon National Park.

# SIERRA PRESS, INC.

4988 Gold Leaf Drive, Mariposa, CA 95338

# CONTENTS

Boat Mesa and Aquarius Plateau from Sunset Point, winter morning.

# BRYCE CANYON
### NATIONAL PARK

**Essay by
Nicky Leach**

Rock and water. A strange alchemy. One apparently static; the other rarely still. In the dry, overheated southwestern landscape—barely moistened by its often ephemeral rivers, creeks, and rainfall—it seems impossible that water could be anything but a bit player in Nature's great show, while rock takes center stage.

Yet nothing could be farther from the truth. The Southwest may be arid, but its elevated plateaus, peaked mountains, great basins, and valleys ensure that the weather has a dramatic impact on these surroundings. Winter storms bring blankets of snow that decorate red rocks and make much of the high country impassable; freeze-thaw cycles of ice and snow wedge open joints in seemingly smooth-faced rocks and hasten erosion; and spring snowmelt and summer rainfall come in dramatic bursts, transforming washes, waterfalls, and rivers into powerful forces.

"Cap" rocks in the Hat Shop.

The presence of water does more than allow plants and animals to retain a precarious foothold; it has actually given birth to and shaped the land—making water both medium and sculptor for the bare, angular sedimentary rocks that are the leitmotif of Canyon Country. At Bryce Canyon National Park, this dual role of water is particularly apparent. Here, forged in a high plateau of geologically recent, uplifted lake deposits, rain, streams, ice, snow, and wind have chiseled a series of unusual, ornately carved amphitheaters in the eastern face of the Paunsaugunt Plateau.

## BORN IN WATER, RAISED IN FIRE

Bryce seems to have more etched columns, spires, windows, balanced rocks, arches, natural bridges, and bizarre "hoodoos" than could ever be counted. The frozen statuary marches out of the soft, sunset-hued rocks of the Claron Formation and forms deep ranks where the sharp-edged plateau drops steeply down to the valley of the Paria River below. Yet this timeless tableau is relatively new, geologically speaking—a consequence of events that started here roughly 65 million years ago.

The crumbly Claron Formation— often referred to as the Pink Cliffs for the large quantities of iron and manganese that give it its trademark hues—is one of the youngest sedimentary rocks in southwestern Utah. It was laid down as silts, sands, and the limy skeletal accretions of dying marine creatures in lagoons and ephemeral freshwater lakes. The lakes were trapped by highlands, which began to be pushed

up when violent seismic activity off the present California coast reverberated eastward, beginning 65 million years ago, building the Sierra Nevada and the Rocky Mountains. Eventually, a 130,000-square-mile geological province (later dubbed the Colorado Plateau for the mighty river in its midst) gradually began to be squeezed, slightly tilted, and broadly uplifted more than a mile high. Faults appeared or reactivated as the earth movements continued.

Locally, the pressure seems to have reached breaking point approximately 13 million years ago, when violent movements along north-south–trending faults pushed the Paunsaugunt and neighboring Markagunt and Aquarius plateaus one above the other into a series of 8,000- to 11,000-foot plateaus (the Aquarius, just east of the Paunsaugunt, is the highest plateau in North America). The Paunsaugunt Plateau, which was raised by the Sevier Fault and dropped along the Paunsaugunt, reaches 9,000 feet in elevation. Nevertheless, its pink, south-facing cliffs are considered the top "step" in what is often termed the Grand Staircase: a series of plateaus rising one above the other from the Grand Canyon to Bryce Canyon, each step composed of rock strata of a different color— in order, the Brown, Vermilion, White, Gray, and finally, the Pink Cliffs of Bryce. Seismic activity continues along these faults, especially the Hurricane Fault, west of the Markagunt Plateau, parallel to Interstate 15. From Bryce, you can see where basalts (less than a million years old) covered the lake sediments atop the 10,000-foot Markagunt.

## NATURE'S MOUNT RUSHMORE

Bryce emerged as weathering began to take its toll on the exposed Claron rocks. Most of what you see is the result of scouring of soft siltstones and harder limestones by runoff from snowmelt and rainfall. The constant weathering by water of rocks of different compositions and hardnesses gives Bryce its many eerie formations, commonly called "hoodoos." The wedging action of frost, which is particularly active along joints in the fragile rocks, enlarges holes from opposite sides of the rocks until they join and break into "windows." The erosive force of water also exposes, and deposits, iron and manganese minerals in, and on, the surface of rocks, coloring the pale strata with reds, pinks, yellows, browns, and purples.

Bryce's greatest appeal has perhaps always been that its fanciful formations unlock our imaginations. Here, as elsewhere in the West, the romantic notions, historical associations, and varied personalities of more than a century of visitors are revealed in the names they attached to landforms that were unlike anything they had ever seen before: Wall Street, The Queen's Garden, Queen Victoria, Thor's Hammer, the Hat Shop, Fairyland, Boat Mesa—some of the monikers are as unlikely as the landscape. Others reflect the Paiute Indian heritage of the area, with such names as Yovimpa, Paunsaugunt, and Markagunt. Still others, such as Sunset, Sunrise, and Rainbow points, need little explanation; their simplicity mirrors the ineffable beauty of the place.

The 19th-century explorer Captain Clarence E. Dutton, whose descriptions of the high plateaus of Utah still make compelling reading, was struck by "the resemblances to strict architectural forms...all (suggest) the work of giant hands, a race of genii, once rearing temples of rock, but now chained up in a spell of enchantment, while their structures are falling in ruins through centuries of decay."

Dutton's theory of "enchantment" is surprisingly like that of the Paiute Indians, who used the land seasonally for many centuries. In 1936, Indian Dick, a Paiute living in the area, told the following story about how Bryce came into existence: *Before there were any Indians, the Legend People, To-when-an-ung-wa, lived in that place. ...Because they were bad, Coyote turned them all into rocks. You can see them in that place now; some standing in rows; some sitting down; some holding onto others. You can see their faces, with paint on them, just as they were before they became rocks....The name of that place is Agka-ku-wass-a-wits (Red Painted Faces).*

Aspens, early autumn.

## BRYCE'S IRRESISTIBLE ALLURE

Bryce Canyon is one of the more unusual attractions in an enormous, untamed area of the West renowned for its scenery. To the east lies the maze of canyons within Canyonlands National Park, the thousands of natural spans of Arches National Park, and the great bulge of the Waterpocket Fold preserved within Capitol Reef National Park. To the southwest, the smooth sandstone "temples and towers" of Zion National Park soar precipitously 2,000 feet skyward, and to the south, the mile-deep gash of the Grand Canyon still forms the focal point for the region.

But for most people, Bryce Canyon National Park is a must. Like Dutton, they come to be "enchanted," and with 25 miles of paved road, numerous scenic pullouts, a host of heart-pumping hikes that descend more than 1,500 feet into the canyon, and a pleasant summer climate, it's not too tall an order. Each season has its magic in this year-round park, offering a peek at Nature's cycle against a remarkable backdrop.

daisies, asters, and other composites in August and September. The tilted, fleshy leaves of boulder-hugging manzanita make up formal-looking gardens beneath an evergreen canopy of pinyon and ponderosa pine, blue spruce, white fir, as the 6,600- to 9,100-foot Paunsaugunt Plateau gradually gains in elevation from north to south. Isolated stands of limber pine and rare bristlecone pine populate exposed, windswept ridges, their adaptation to the harsh margin allowing them to survive for thousands of years under the right conditions. Warm temperatures bring back mule deer that have wintered at lower elevations. They are regularly seen by visitors as they contentedly browse alongside the road in the early evening, perhaps being watched at the same time from a discreet distance by rarely seen mountain lions. Water pours along tributaries to the Paria River below, cutting gullies through rainbow-washed rocks and deterring plant growth. The naked hoodoos offer a complete contrast to the verdant mesa top.

By summer, the park is in full swing. Rangers try to answer a million questions at once; busy campgrounds ring with laughter and many different languages; ranger talks, moonlit walks, scenic drives, and the shorter hikes below the rim through the spectacular carved rocks of Queen's Garden and Navajo Loop are popular activities. The park's longest hike, the Under-the-Rim Trail, beckons backcountry hikers. Ground squirrels beg shamelessly at picnic tables (but no matter how

Although some south-facing exposures warm up enough by late March or early April to fast forward nature's clock, spring is usually a latecomer in the rugged high country. Temperatures in cool, shaded plateau areas go up around the beginning of May and melt the deep snows. The runoff sets the stage for sprays of penstemons, skyrocket gilia, Indian paintbrush, and lavender-hued lupines to emerge in June and July, followed by cute they may seem, don't be lured into giving hand-outs; feeding park animals is not allowed—for their good and yours). Swallows swoop along the cliffs; while hawks and ravens carry out aerial maneuvers above. As summer changes to autumn nights are crisper and longer, and an air of anticipation hangs over Bryce. Frost gives way to ice. At lower elevations, pinyon trees drop their precious nuts. Smoke trickles up from the valley below. Snowflakes tease the air.

Winter is perhaps the most pure experience one can have of Bryce Canyon. Although the visitor center remains active, other buildings lie hushed and deserted. Snow-laden roads are plowed and sanded, but above-the-rim trails are not and often must be negotiated using snowshoes and cross-country skis. Below the rim, snow and ice frequently make the trails nearly inaccessible. Then, one can only gaze at the beauty. Trees and rocks, blanketed with white powder, seem silent and magical at twilight, fantastical in the thin, frozen air of daytime. One under-subscribed campground loop stays open for hardy campers willing to look to their own resources. In winter, time seems to stand still in Bryce, as if no one else had ever been here.

## BADLAND OR PROMISED LAND?

Before Clarence Dutton's 1880 survey trip throughout the remote canyons and plateaus of the Grand Canyon region, Bryce Canyon's magnificent scenery had received very little attention. In 1874, the Paria Valley began to be used by Mormon colonists like Ebenezer

Bryce, who, along with fellow Mormon settlers, raised livestock and crops at the base of these cliffs. Bryce moved before a ditch diverting water from the East Fork of the Sevier River could be constructed, making the tiny new farming community of Tropic possible in 1892. (The ditch can still be seen today along the trail in Water Canyon and from atop the plateau.) These pioneers appear to have had little laudatory to say about the dry, high-relief country they found themselves in—it was Ebenezer Bryce who is said to have remarked that it was awful hard to find a cow that was lost in the canyon that came to bear his name.

A thousand years before the arrival of Mormon settlers, Anasazi and Fremont Indians ventured to these highlands in summer to hunt deer, elk, rabbits, and other game and to gather important plants for food, medicine, and clothing. The plateau was too cold for year-round living, so these cultures maintained residences and small fields of crops in the warmer valleys the rest of the year. When the Fremont disappeared as a culture and the Anasazi moved south to more reliable farmlands, starting in the 1200s, a largely peripatetic culture, known as the Paiute, entered the picture. Their influence may still be felt throughout southern Utah, where place names reflect the Paiute's familiarity with the important characteristics of their adopted homeland: Markagunt Plateau (Highland of Trees), Paunsaugunt Plateau (Home of the Beaver), the Paria (Muddy Water) River, the nearby town of Panguitch (Big

Glow of light through a window in Seal Castle.

Fish), and many others.

## THE TEMPLE OF THE GODS

Word about Bryce Canyon was slow to get out, but when the area was made part of a new forest preserve in 1905, news began to leak back East. The lack of roads to the remote plateau continued to be a deterrent to travel, but in 1915, the canyon got a boost when a new forest supervisor, J. W. (Will) Humphrey, was engaged. Humphrey was immediately smitten with the canyon and secured funds for a rough road to the plateau. He wrote glowing descriptions about Bryce Canyon and invited people to view it for themselves. In 1916, he received help when a local rancher, Ruby Syrett, and his family built a ranch house just outside the present park and began exploring the rim. So taken were the Syretts with the place that they, as well as Humphrey's employer (the U.S. Forest Service), began enthusiastically promoting the canyon and hosting journalists and other visitors. Articles in the *Salt Lake Tribune* and *Scientific American,* both in 1918, proclaimed "Utah's New Wonderland, Bryce's Canyon" and "The Temple of the Gods in Utah." In 1920, the Syretts built a lodge, Tourist Rest, near the rim, and guests "registered" by carving their names in the big wooden double doors of the hostelry.

Efforts by the State of Utah to have Bryce Canyon set aside as Temple of the Gods National Monument met with resistance at the federal level. Finally, political pressure prevailed, and Bryce was accorded national monument status in 1923. The Union Pacific Railroad (UPR) lost no time in buying out Ruby Syrett and creating a tourist circuit that brought travelers by bus from Cedar City through the scenic attractions of southern Utah, putting them up in specially built "rustic" lodges at Bryce, Cedar Breaks, Zion, and the Grand Canyon.

Today, Bryce Canyon Lodge, with its surrounding log cabins, heavy timber construction, great windows, and wavy-shingled roof, is the last of the original park lodges designed by architect Gilbert Stanley Underwood for UPR. (Those at Grand Canyon and Zion were either damaged or destroyed by fire and later rebuilt; the Cedar Breaks Lodge was pulled down in the 1970s.) The historic lodge at Bryce Canyon was restored by the National Park Service between 1987 and 1991 and usually remains full until it closes in winter. Ruby's Inn, outside the park entrance, is still run by the grandchildren of Ruby Syrett, although, today, Bryce Canyon's first hoteliers have plenty of competition from neighboring businesses serving visitors to the park.

## NO "PARK" IS AN ISLAND UNTO ITSELF...

Bryce Canyon was finally afforded national park status by Congress in 1928 and has gradually expanded to accommodate its present fifty-six square miles. More than 1.6 million people visited Bryce Canyon in 1993. In peak season, the large number of visitors occasionally slows traffic on the scenic drive and keeps Bryce Canyon Lodge and the two small campgrounds within the park hopping with activity. Development of some areas just outside park boundaries is also a constant threat to the integrity of the fragile ecosystem preserved within the park. An attempt to start up a coal mining operation at nearby Alton was averted in 1980, after park officials and other concerned groups and individuals raised questions about the effects such development would have on the adjoining park. In addition, issues of noise from air and highway traffic, waste disposal, water reclamation, access to land leases, air quality, and a diminishing aquifer all affect the park.

For many years, Bryce Canyon was isolated and difficult to reach, but with the advent of all-weather, paved roads in southern Utah, the park has become all too accessible. In 1994, expecting increased traffic congestion due to road construction on the last seven miles of the narrow scenic drive, the National Park Service instigated an experimental optional shuttle system, allowing visitors to leave their cars outside the park and ride to viewpoints. Similar systems are in use at Grand Canyon's South Rim and have been experimented with in Zion National Park. Should visitation, and traffic congestion, continue to increase in the future such a system may become a regular option for visitors.

Bryce Canyon's historic airport, which was built five miles outside the park by the Civilian Conservation Corps in the 1930s, has been popular since it was built. It has been used extensively as a rural airport stopover and has seen its share of tragedy. In 1947, a VC10 flying between Los Angeles and Chicago went down in the northern end of the park, killing fifty three people and prompting new air safety regulations.

Bryce Canyon is just one of many fascinating stops along Utah's one hundred and twenty-mile Highway 12 Scenic Byway. Consistently cited as one of America's most scenic routes, it begins at the junction of Highways 12 and 89, just west of Red Canyon (a rival to Bryce for beauty and popularity), and ends at Highway 24, just outside Capitol Reef National Park in the east. Interpretive markers prepared by a workgroup made up of local, state, and federal agencies, including the National Park Service, offer geological, historical, and natural history information at pull-outs along the highway. Such cooperative efforts underscore the fact that Bryce Canyon is no longer a remote outpost, but an important thread in the finely woven tapestry of scenic places that make up this spectacular area of the country.

Cloud floating above Wall of Windows.

# BRYCE CANYON
### NATIONAL PARK

## A VISUAL
## INTERPRETATION

A section of Queen's Garden seen from Sunrise Point.

"The Hunter", Agua Canyon.

The view into Bryce Amphitheater from Inspiration Point.

Afternoon storm seen from Agua Canyon viewpoint.     16

Winter sunrise illuminates Bryce Amphitheater.

Douglas fir growing from the depths of Wall Street.                18

The view from Rainbow Point, summer afternoon.

Rolling hills of the Claron Formation near Boat Mesa.     20

Towers and hoodoos in Fairyland Canyon.

The Silent City, late-afternoon, winter.

23      The Queen's Garden seen from Sunrise Point, early morning.

Hoodoos silhouetted at sunrise, Navajo Loop Trail.          24

Tower glowing in late-afternoon light.

Bryce Amphitheater seen from Bryce Point.

Ponderosa pines in fog and snow.

Snow-capped formations in the Silent City.

Bryce Amphitheater seen from the Peekaboo Trail.

The Silent City in backlight seen from Sunset Point.  30

Fog and snow seen from Bryce Point, winter.

Thor's Hammer and Temple of Osiris, winter afternoon.

Colorful slope eroding between Sunrise and Sunset Points.

The striated grain of a Utah juniper.

35    Meadow grasses atop the plateau at Bryce Canyon, mid-summer.

Yovimpa Point, winter sunset.

Winter sunrise from Sunset Point.

Campbell Canyon seen from the Fairyland Loop Trail.          38

Bryce Amphitheater, sunrise from Sunrise Point.

Hoodoos in Queen's Garden seen from Sunset Point.

Hoodoos seen from the Queen's Garden Trail.

Ponderosa pines and aspens, autumn.

43      Bryce Amphitheater framed by a tunnel on the Peekaboo Trail.

Bristlecone pines surviving on a nearly barren slope. 44

Thor's Hammer seen from the Navajo Loop Trail, sunrise.

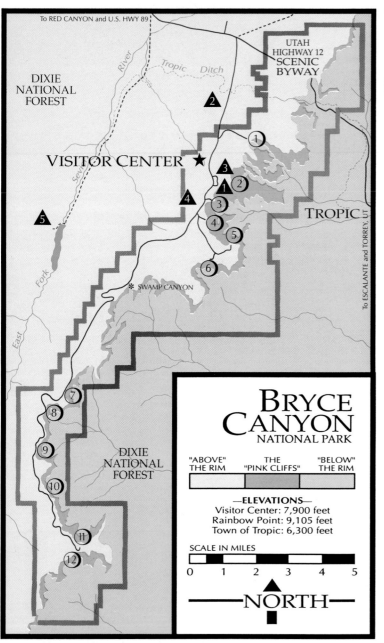

# BRYCE CANYON
## NATIONAL PARK

## VIEW POINTS (North to South)

1. Fairyland Point
2. Sunrise Point
3. Sunset Point
4. Inspiration Point
5. Bryce Point
6. Paria View
7. Farview Point
8. Natural Bridge
9. Agua Canyon
10. Ponderosa Canyon Viewpoint
11. Rainbow Point
12. Yovimpa Point

## ACCOMODATIONS

1. Bryce Canyon Lodge (Seasonal)
2. Ruby's Inn (Year-round)
3. North Campground (Year-round)
4. Sunset Campground (Seasonal)
5. King's Creek Campground (USFS)

## PARK INFORMATION

Superintendent
**Bryce Canyon NP**
Bryce Canyon, UT 84717
(801) 834-5322

**Bryce Canyon NHA**
Bryce Canyon National Park
Bryce Canyon, UT 84717
(801) 834-5322

**Bryce Canyon Lodge**
PO Box 400
Cedar City, UT 84721
(801) 586-7686

**Ruby's Inn**
Bryce, UT 84764
(801) 834-5341
(800) 528-1234

# Bryce Canyon National Park

**Bryce Canyon National Park** is located near the center of the greatest concentration of National Parks, Monuments, and Recreation Areas in the United States. Although the temptation is great, don't make the mistake of trying to see too much in too little time—rather, take your time and experience your destination fully. It is far more satisfying to completely see one area than to catch only an incomplete glimpse of five or six. Take the time to enjoy this magnificent landscape, you'll be glad you did!

## REGIONAL ATTRACTIONS

- (A) Arches National Park
- (B) Canyon deChelly Nat'l Monument (NM)
- (C) Canyonlands NP
- (D) Capitol Reef NP
- (E) Cedar Breaks NM
- (F) Colorado NM
- (G) Dinosaur NM
- (H) Glen Canyon National Recreation Area (NRA)
- (I) Grand Canyon NP
- (J) Great Basin NP
- (K) Hovenweep NM
- (L) Hubbell Trading Post Nat'l Historic Site
- (M) Lake Mead NRA
- (N) Mesa Verde NP
- (O) Montezuma Castle NM
- (P) Monument Valley Tribal Park, Az.
- (Q) Natural Bridges NM
- (R) Navajo NM
- (S) Petrified Forest NP
- (T) Pipe Spring NM
- (U) Rainbow Bridge NM
- (V) Tuzigoot NM
- (W) Valley of Fire State Park
- (X) Walnut Canyon NM
- (Y) Wupatki & Sunset Crater NM
- (Z) Zion NP

## REGIONAL INFORMATION

**Dixie Nat'l Forest**
82 North 100 East
Cedar City, UT 84720
(801) 865-3700

**Garfield County Travel Council**
PO Box 200
Panguitch, UT 84759
(800) 444-6689

**Utah Travel Council**
Council Hall/Capitol Hill
Salt Lake City, UT 84118
(801) 538-1030

**Escalante Interagency Office**
PO Box 246
Escalante, UT 84726
(801) 826-5499

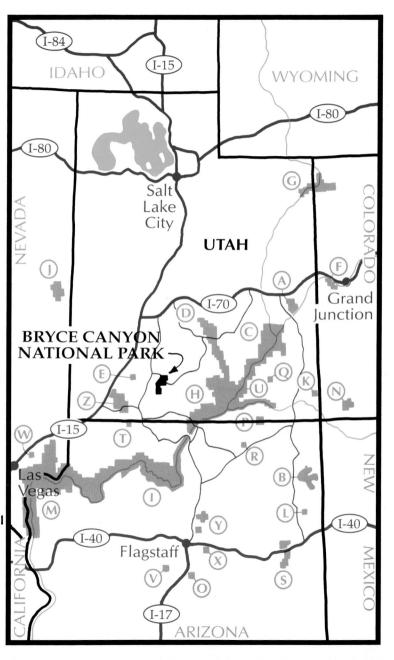

# SUGGESTED READING

**Bezy, John**. *Bryce Canyon: The Story Behind the Scenery*. Las Vegas, NV: KC Publications, Inc. 1982.

**Bruhn, Arthur**. *Exploring Southern Utah's Land of Color*. Revised and updated by Nicky Leach. Springdale, UT: Zion Natural History Association. 1993.

**Buchanan, Dr. Hayle**. *Wildflowers of Southwestern Utah*. Bryce Canyon, UT: Bryce Canyon Natural History Association. 1992.

**DeCourten, Frank**. *Shadows of Time: The Geology of Bryce Canyon National Park*. Bryce Canyon, UT: Bryce Canyon Natural History Association. 1994.

*Desert Southwest*. The Sierra Club Guides to the National Parks. New York, NY: Stewart, Tabori, and Chang. 1984.

**Euler, Robert C**. *Southern Paiute Ethnohistory*. Anthropological Papers, No. 78. Salt Lake City, UT: University of Utah. 1966.

**Leach, Nicky**. *The Guide to National Parks of the Southwest*. Tucson, AZ: Southwest Parks & Monuments Association. 1992.

**Woodbury, Angus**. *A History of Southern Utah and Its National Parks*. Salt Lake City, UT: Utah State Historical Society. 1944. Revised Edition, 1950.

# CREDITS

"Bryce Canyon National Park" essay by Nicky Leach.
Edited by Rose Houk.
Book Design by Jeff Nicholas.
Photo Editor: Jeff Nicholas.
All maps by Jeff Nicholas.
Printing coordinated by TWP, Ltd., Berkeley, Ca.
Printed in Singapore, 1995.

# PHOTOGRAPHIC CREDITS

**Gail Bandini:** 23
**Russ Bishop:** 31
**Bob Clemenz:** 42
**Carr Clifton:** 8
**Ed Cooper:** 30
**Charles Cramer:** 15(Right)
**Tom Danielsen:** 32
**R. Todd Davis:** 9,15(Left)
**Dick Dietrich:** 6
**Jack W. Dykinga:** 2,22
**Craig Fucile:** 21
**Jeff Gnass:** 19,40
**Jenny Hager:** 12,13,34
**Fred Hirschmann:** 28,33,41,44
**D. A. Horchner:** 11,20
**George H. Huey:** 10
**Gary Ladd:** 25,29,43
**Jeff Nicholas:** Front Cover, Back Cover
**Pat O'Hara:** 27
**James Randklev:** 3(Left),14,35
**Lee Rentz (Bruce Coleman, Inc.):** 16
**Randall K. Roberts:** 18
**Tom Till:** 17
**Larry Ulrich:** 3(Right),24,26,38
**Glenn Van Nimwegen:** 7,37
**Jim Wilson:** 39,45
**George Wuerthner:** 36